Let's Get Cooking

CLEAN EATING

Over **100** wholesome recipes

igloobooks

Published in 2017
by Igloo Books Ltd
Cottage Farm
Sywell
NN6 0BJ
www.igloobooks.com

Designed by Nicholas Gage
Edited by Jasmin Peppiatt

All imagery: © iStock / Getty Images

REX001 0617
2 4 6 8 10 9 7 5 3 1
ISBN 978-1-78670-479-5

Printed and manufactured in China

Contents

Breakfasts

Banana and Almond Smoothie

2 bananas, sliced
500 ml / 17 ½ fl. oz / 2 cups almond milk
1 tbsp runny honey

1. Spread the banana slices out on a baking tray and freeze for at least 2 hours. They can then be stored in a freezer bag for later use or used straight away.
2. Put the frozen banana in a liquidizer with the almond milk and honey and blend until very smooth.
3. Pour into two glasses and serve immediately.

Berry Smoothie Bowl

50 g / 1 ¾ oz / ¼ cup chia seeds
28 g buckwheat porridge flakes
500 ml / 17 ½ fl. oz / 2 cups almond milk
150 g / 5 ½ oz / 1 cup frozen
    summer berries
2 tbsp maple syrup

TO GARNISH
1 handful fresh berries
2 tbsp goji berries
2 tbsp chia seeds
2 tbsp pumpkin seeds
2 tbsp sunflower seeds

1. Stir the chia seeds and buckwheat flakes into the almond milk and leave to thicken for 20 minutes.
2. Transfer to a liquidizer and add the berries and maple syrup and blend until very smooth.
3. Pour into two bowls and arrange the berries and seeds on top.

SERVES: **6** | PREP TIME: **5 MINS** | COOKING TIME: **1 HOUR**

Hazelnut and Cherry Granola

75 ml / 2 ½ fl. oz / ⅓ cup maple syrup
75 ml / 2 ½ fl. oz / ⅓ cup white grape juice
1 tbsp linseed oil
175 g / 6 oz / 1 ¾ cups rolled buckwheat flakes
100 g / 3 ½ oz / ¾ cup hazelnuts
75 g / 2 ½ oz / ⅔ cup almonds
100 g / 3 ½ oz / 1 cup sunflower seeds
150 g / 5 ½ oz / ¾ cup dried sour cherries
75 g / 2 ½ oz / ⅓ cup sultanas
soya yogurt to serve

1. Preheat the oven to 160°C (140°C fan) / 325F / gas 3.
2. Stir the maple syrup, grape juice and oil together in a bowl with a pinch of salt then toss it with the buckwheat flakes, hazelnuts, almonds and sunflower seeds.
3. Spread the mixture out on a large baking tray and bake for 1 hour, stirring every 10 minutes to ensure it all toasts evenly. Leave the granola to cool completely, then stir in the sour cherries and sultanas.
4. Store in an airtight jar until needed, then serve with soya yogurt.

Coconut Cacao Smoothie

50 g / 1 ¾ oz / ¼ cup chia seeds
25 g desiccated coconut
500 ml / 17 ½ fl. oz / 2 cups coconut water
2 bananas, sliced and frozen for at least 2 hours
2 tbsp pure cacao powder
2 tbsp dried coconut flakes
2 tbsp cocoa nibs

1. Stir the chia seeds and desiccated coconut into the coconut water and leave to thicken for 20 minutes.
2. Transfer to a liquidizer with the bananas and cacao powder and blend until very smooth.
3. Pour into two glasses or jars and top each one with a spoonful of coconut flakes and a spoonful of cocoa nibs.

Strawberry Yogurt with Granola

300 g / 10.5 oz / 2 cups fresh strawberries
2 tsp low calorie sweetener powder
500 g / 1 lb 2 oz fat-free Greek yogurt
1 lemon, juiced
100 g / 3.5 oz / ¾ cup low sugar granola
fresh mint to garnish

1. Slice just 3 or 4 strawberries then set aside. Place the rest of the strawberries and the low calorie sweetener powder into a blender and pulse until coarsely chopped and combined.

2. Mix the lemon juice into the yogurt and add to the strawberry puree in the blender. Blend gently to combine. Taste to check balance of sweetness and add further low calorie sweetener if required.

3. Place some of the granola into a small glass tumbler before adding the sliced strawberries and the yogurt mix. Layer as desired saving some of the granola for the top and garnish with fresh mint.

4. Great for a quick healthy breakfast and can be made in a mason jar for breakfast on the go.

Mean Green Juice

2 sticks celery, chopped

150 g / 5 ½ oz / 1 cup apples, peeled, cored and cubed

150 g / 5 ½ oz / 1 cup green seedless grapes

35 g spinach

35 g flat-leaf parsley

500 ml / 18 fl. oz / 2 cups apple juice

1 lemon, juiced

1. Spread the celery, apple and grapes out on a greaseproof paper lined baking tray and freeze for at least 2 hours. It can then be transferred to a freezer bag and stored for future use or used straight away.

2. Put the spinach and parsley in a liquidizer with the apple juice and lemon juice. Blend until smooth.

3. Add the frozen celery, apple and grapes and blend again until smooth, then pour into glasses and serve immediately.

SERVES: **1** | PREP TIME: **10 MINS**

Granola Fruit Yogurt Bowl

100 g / 3 ½ oz fresh raspberries
100 g /3 ½ oz fresh blackberries
250 g / 8 oz / 1 cup organic yogurt
1 tsp raw honey
1 small banana, sliced
30 g granola
2 strawberries, sliced
½ mango, sliced
15 g coconut flakes

1. Place the fresh berries into a blender and blitz into a puree.
2. Strain through a fine sieve into a bowl to remove any seeds and skins.
3. Mix the yogurt and honey into the berries so that you have a fresh yogurt base for the bowl.
4. Top the yogurt with the remaining ingredients for a fresh and fruity breakfast.

Raspberry and Oat Smoothie

150 g / 5 ½ oz / 1 cup raspberries
300 ml / 10 ½ fl. oz / 1 ¼ cups almond milk
50 g / 1 ¾ oz / ½ cup rolled porridge oats, plus extra for sprinkling
1 tbsp runny honey

1. Spread out the raspberries on a baking tray that has been lined with greaseproof paper and freeze for at least 2 hours.
2. Meanwhile, put the almond milk and oats in a liquidizer and leave to soak.
3. When the raspberries are ready, transfer them to the liquidizer with the honey and blend until smooth.
4. Pour into two jars or glasses and serve with a sprinkle of oats on top.

Blueberry Smoothie

150 g / 5 ½ oz / 1 cup blueberries

100 g / 3 ½ oz / ½ cup silken tofu

350 ml / 12 fl. oz / 1 ½ cups pure
blueberry juice

1 tbsp runny honey

2 sprigs mint

1. Reserve a few blueberries for garnish
then spread the rest out on a baking
tray and freeze for at least 2 hours.
They can then be stored in a freezer
bag for later use or used straight away.

2. Put the frozen blueberries in a
liquidizer with the tofu, juice and
honey and blend until very smooth.

3. Pour into two glasses, garnish with
blueberries and mint and
serve immediately.

Avocado Spinach Smoothie

2 ripe avocados, skinned,
  stoned and chopped
1 banana, chopped
35 g / 1 cup baby leaf spinach
250 ml / 9 fl. oz / 1 cup soya milk
½ lemon, juiced

1. Spread the avocado and banana out on a greaseproof paper lined baking tray and freeze for at least 2 hours. It can then be transferred to a freezer bag and stored for future use or used straight away.
2. Put the spinach in a liquidizer with the soya milk and lemon juice. Blend until smooth.
3. Add the frozen avocado and banana and blend again until smooth, then pour into two glasses and serve immediately.

Quinoa Granola

75 ml / 2 ½ fl. oz / ⅓ cup runny honey
75 ml / 2 ½ fl. oz / ⅓ cup apple juice
1 tbsp extra virgin olive oil
175 g / 6 oz / 1 ¾ cups rolled porridge oats
100 g / 3 ½ oz / ¾ cup almonds,
  roughly chopped
75 g / 2 ½ oz / ½ cup quinoa
50 g / 1 ¾ oz / ½ cup sunflower seeds
200 g / 7 oz / 1 cup goji berries
10 medjool dates, stoned and chopped

1. Preheat the oven to 160°C (140°C fan) / 325F / gas 3.
2. Stir the honey, apple juice and oil together in a bowl with a pinch of salt then toss it with the oats, almonds, quinoa and sunflower seeds.
3. Spread the mixture out on a large baking tray and bake for 1 hour, stirring every 10 minutes to ensure it all toasts evenly. Leave the granola to cool completely, then stir in the goji berries and dates.
4. Store in an airtight jar until needed.

Matcha and Chia Smoothie

50 g / 1 ¾ oz / ¼ cup chia seeds
1 tbsp matcha green tea powder
600 ml / 1 pint / 2 ½ cups soya milk
2 bananas, sliced and frozen for
    at least 2 hours
2 tbsp maple syrup
1 tbsp goji berries

1. Stir the chia seeds and matcha into the soya milk and leave to thicken for 20 minutes.
2. Transfer to a liquidizer with the bananas and maple syrup and blend until smooth.
3. Pour into two glasses and serve immediately, garnished with goji berries.

Acai Superfood Bowl

100 g / 3 ½ oz unsweetened Acai purée,
    frozen sachet
½ banana, sliced
50 g / 1 ¾ oz fresh blueberries
50 g / 1 ¾ oz fresh strawberries
60 ml / 2 fl. oz coconut milk
1 tsp chia seeds
1 tsp flax seeds
1 tsp pumpkin seeds
1 tsp bee pollen
1 tsp granola
30 g coconut flakes

1. Run the frozen Acai sachet under a warm tap, cut open and break into a blender. Add the banana, blueberries, strawberries and a splash of coconut milk and blend. Continue to gradually add the rest of the coconut milk and blend until the mixture has combined into a thick smoothie.
2. Pour into a bowl and top with the other ingredients, adding a drizzle of agave syrup if desired.

Cinnamon Toasted Oats with Yogurt

300 g / 10 ½ oz / 3 cups whole rolled oats

50 g / 1 ¾ oz / ½ cup pumpkin seeds

50 g / 1 ¾ oz / ½ cup sunflower seeds

100 g / 3 oz / 1 cup whole almonds

1 tsp cinnamon

1 tsp vanilla extract

1 tsp water

100 g / 3 oz / ½ cup dried fruits e.g. sultanas, apricot, raisins

250 g / 8 ½ oz 0 per cent fat organic yogurt

2 tsp fruit syrup

1. Preheat the oven to 200°C (180°C fan) / 400F / gas 6.
2. Spread the oats, seeds and almonds evenly on a baking tray and place into the oven for 5-7 minutes until slightly browned and fragrant.
3. Whilst the oats are in the oven, mix the cinnamon, vanilla and water in a small bowl.
4. Remove the oats from the oven and drizzle over the cinnamon mixture. Toss to coat the oats and place back into the oven for a further 2-3 minutes.
5. Allow to cool, mix with the dried fruits, then store in an airtight container until needed.
6. To serve, fill a bowl with the yogurt and top with the oat mixture before drizzling over the fruit syrup.

Green Smoothie Bowl

3 bananas

3 kiwi fruit, peeled

150 g / 5 ½ oz / 1 cup blueberries

3 green apples, cored and thinly sliced

35 g / 1 cup baby leaf spinach

250 ml / 9 fl. oz / 1 cup coconut milk

2 tbsp maple syrup

1 lime, cut into thin wedges

2 tbsp toasted oats

1 tbsp desiccated coconut

a few sprigs of mint

1. Set aside a banana and a kiwi for the garnish then peel and chop the rest.
2. Spread half the blueberries, two of the sliced apples and the chopped banana and kiwi out on a greaseproof paper lined baking tray and freeze for 2 hours. The fruit can be transferred to a freezer bag and stored for future use or used immediately.
3. Put the spinach in a liquidizer with the coconut milk and maple syrup.
4. Blend until smooth.
5. Add the frozen fruit and blend again until smooth, then pour into two chilled bowls.
6. Cut the final kiwi in half in a zigzag pattern, then peel and slice the final banana.
7. Arrange on top of the smoothie with the blueberries, apple and lime slices, then sprinkle with oats and coconut. Garnish with mint and serve immediately.

Summer Berry Smoothie

1 banana

150 g / 5 oz / 1 cup fresh or
   frozen blackberries

150 g / 5 oz / 1 cup fresh or
   frozen raspberries

250 g / 8 ½ oz / 1 cup non-fat yogurt

1 tsp raw honey or agave syrup

50 g / 1 ½ oz / ¼ cup muesli

fresh berries to garnish

1. Blend all ingredients except the muesli in a blender until smooth. If mixture is a little thick, add some milk.
2. Divide into two cups, sprinkle with the muesli and garnish with halved berries.

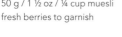

SERVES: **6-8** | PREP TIME: **5 MINS** | COOKING TIME: **20 MINS**

Fresh Granola with Seeds

150 g / 5 ¼ oz / ½ cup pure maple syrup
2 tbsp raw honey
2 tbsp coconut oil
1 tsp vanilla extract
300 g / 10 ½ oz / 3 cups whole rolled oats
100 g / 3 ½ oz / ¾ cup pumpkin seeds
100 g / 3 ½ oz / ¾ cup sunflower seeds
100 g / 3 ½ oz/ ¾ cup pecan pieces
100 g / 3 ½ oz / ½ cup dried cranberries

1. Preheat the oven to 150°C (130°C fan) / 300F / gas 2.
2. Mix together the syrup, honey, oil and vanilla extract in a large bowl. Pour in the remaining ingredients, except the berries, and mix well.
3. Tip the granola mixture onto a baking tray and spread evenly (use two baking trays if required) and place in the oven to bake for 20 minutes, turning the mixture over once during cooking.
4. Remove from the oven and leave to cool.
5. Once cooled, mix in the dried fruits and store in an airtight container for up to 1 month. Serve with fresh berries, yogurt or almond milk.

SERVES: 4 | PREP TIME: 5 MINS | COOKING TIME: 10 MINS

French Toast

4 egg whites, lightly beaten

60 ml / 2 fl. oz almond milk

½ tsp cinnamon

½ tsp nutmeg

1 tsp vanilla extract

1 tsp date sugar

8 slices of wholewheat bread

2 tsp date syrup

1. Combine the egg, milk, cinnamon, nutmeg, vanilla and sugar in a large bowl.

2. Soak the bread in the egg mixture taking care not to let it get too soggy and fry in a non-stick pan over a medium heat for a couple of minutes on each side or until caramelized.

3. Serve with a drizzle of syrup and any other additional toppings of your choice.

Main Meals

SERVES: 2 | PREP TIME: 10 MINS | COOKING TIME: 10 MINS

Stir-fry Chilli Prawns

100 g / 3 ½ oz dried egg noodles

2 tsp vegetable oil

15g ginger, finely chopped
   or grated

2 garlic cloves, finely chopped

1 red chilli (chili), finely diced

200 g / 7 oz raw peeled king prawns

½ red pepper, sliced

½ yellow pepper, sliced

½ green pepper, sliced

30 g cup cashew nuts, chopped

1 lime, juiced

2 tsp of sesame oil

1. Cook the noodles as per the packet instructions, drain, rinse and set aside

2. Heat oil in a wok or large pan. Add the ginger, garlic and chilli and cook for 2 minutes. Add the peppers and prawns and cook for a further 3 minutes until the prawns are pink and cooked through.

3. Return the noodles to the pan and heat through, adding the lime juice, sesame oil and cashew nuts before serving.

SERVES: **2** | PREP TIME: **10 MINS** | COOKING TIME: **30 MINS**

Roasted Pepper with Quinoa

1 red pepper, halved and deseeded
1 yellow pepper, halved and deseeded
150 g / 5 ¼ oz / ¾ cup quinoa
1 tsp extra virgin olive oil
1 lime, juice and zest
sea salt and freshly ground black pepper
1 handful fresh basil leaves
30 g pumpkin seeds

1. Preheat the oven to 230°C (210°C fan) / 450F / gas 8 and place the peppers on a baking tray cut side down. Place in the oven and roast for 25 minutes or until the skin begins to blacken in places.
2. Remove from the oven and leave to cool until you can handle the peppers.
3. Remove the charred skin leaving the tender flesh, which can be chopped into smaller pieces.
4. While the peppers are cooling, cook the quinoa as per the packet instructions and drain well. Sir through the oil and lime before seasoning with the salt and pepper to taste.
5. Mix through the roasted peppers and place into serving bowls before topping with the basil and pumpkin seeds.

SERVES: **2** | PREP TIME: **10 MINS** | COOKING TIME: **15 MINS**

Mediterranean Courgetti

200 g / 7 oz vine-ripened cherry tomatoes
10 g pine nuts
50 g / 1 ¾ oz baby spinach, roughly chopped
30 g fresh basil, roughly chopped
1 garlic clove, crushed
1 lemon, juice and zest
100 ml / 3 ½ fl. oz / ½ cup extra virgin olive oil
sea salt and freshly ground black pepper
500 g / 1 lb 2 oz courgetti
100 g / 3 ½ oz feta cheese

1. Preheat your oven to 180°C (160°C fan) / 350F / gas 4.
2. Place the tomatoes on a baking tray, drizzle with a little oil and season before roasting in the oven for 15 minutes until softened.
3. While the tomatoes are roasting, fry the pine nuts in a dry pan for a minute and place into a food processor with the garlic, spinach, basil and lemon then blend until combined. Gradually pour in the oil whilst continuing to blend to make a pesto. Season to taste and set aside.
4. Bring a pan of salted water to boil on the hob and add the courgetti.
5. Cook for 2-3 minutes until tender, then drain well and return to the pan. Stir in enough of the pesto to coat the courgetti and transfer to warmed plates.
6. Add the roasted tomatoes then crumble over the feta cheese and some torn basil leaves.

SERVES: 4-6 | PREP TIME: 10 MINS | COOKING TIME: 15 MINS

Herby Quinoa Salad

300 g / 10 ½ oz / 1 ½ cups quinoa

1 red onion, finely sliced

1 small bunch of flat leaf
parsley, chopped

1 small bunch of coriander, chopped

1 small bunch of fresh mint, chopped

2 lemons, zested and juiced

sea salt and freshly ground black pepper

1. Cook the quinoa as per the packet instructions.

2. Drain the quinoa thoroughly and spread over a baking tray to cool quickly and steam dry.

3. Once the quinoa has cooled, mix together with the other ingredients in a serving bowl and season with salt and black pepper.

4. Serve immediately.

MAKES: **2** | PREP TIME: **15 MINS** | COOKING TIME: **20 MINS**

Red Quinoa with Vegetables

100 g / 3 ½ oz / ½ cup red quinoa

200 g / 7 oz broccoli, cooked and drained

1 tsp capers

1 tsp pumpkin seeds

100 g / 3 ½ oz / ½ cup sun-dried tomatoes

100 g / 100 g baby spinach, washed and dried

1 lemon, juiced

1 tsp Dijon mustard

1 garlic clove, crushed

30 ml extra virgin olive oil

sea salt and freshly ground black pepper

1. Place the quinoa into a saucepan with water, 2 parts liquid to 1 part quinoa, and bring to the boil. Reduce to a simmer, cover and cook for 15 minutes. Drain well and set aside to cool.

2. Once the quinoa has cooled, mix the broccoli, capers, pumpkin seeds and tomatoes into the quinoa and season to taste.

3. Place the baby spinach at the bottom of a serving bowl and top with the quinoa mixture.

4. To make the dressing, whisk together the lemon, mustard and garlic before gradually adding the oil until it forms a slightly thick and creamy consistency.

5. Season to taste and drizzle over the quinoa salad before serving.

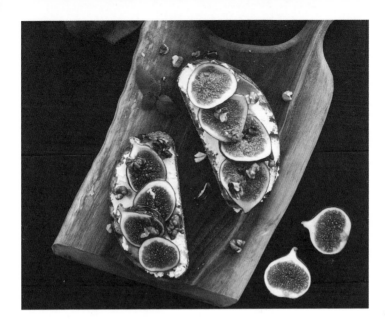

SERVES: **1** | PREP TIME: **10 MINS**

Figs and Ricotta with Honey

100 g / 3 ½ oz low fat ricotta cheese
3 tsp date syrup
4 fresh figs, halved
20 g cup walnuts, chopped
2 slices of toasted sour dough

1. Stir half of the date syrup into the ricotta and spread onto the toast.
2. Arrange the halved figs on top of the ricotta and drizzle over the remaining syrup.
3. Sprinkle over the walnut pieces and serve.

SERVES: 4 | PREP TIME: 20 MINS | COOKING TIME: 55 MINS

Chia Crispbread Sandwiches

FOR THE CRISPBREADS
75 g / 2 ½ oz / ⅓ cup chia seeds
75 g / 2 ½ oz / ⅓ cup golden
  linseeds seeds
75 g / 2 ½ oz / ⅓ cup sesame seeds
50 g / 1 ¾ oz / ½ cup ground almonds
1 tsp herbes de Provence

FOR THE FILLING
100 g / 3 ½ oz / ½ cup hummus
100 g / 3 ½ oz / ½ cup vegan pesto
1 large handful rocket (arugula)
1 red pepper, sliced
35 g / 1 ¼ oz / 1 cup alfalfa sprouts
2 tbsp pine nuts, toasted
3 spring onions (scallions), chopped

1. Preheat the oven to 160°C (140°C fan) / 325F / gas 3 and line a large baking tray with greaseproof paper.
2. Mix all of the crispbread ingredients in a bowl with ¼ tsp salt, then stir in 250 ml of cold water. When all of the water has been absorbed, spread it onto the baking tray in an even 5 mm thick layer.
3. Bake the crispbread sheet for 30 minutes. Cut it into eight even rectangles, turn them over with a spatula, then return the tray to the oven and bake for 25 minutes or until dry and crisp. Leave to cool on the tray.
4. Spread half of the crispbreads with hummus and the other half with pesto.
5. Top the hummus breads with rocket, pepper, alfalfa sprouts, pine nuts and spring onions, then invert the pesto crispbreads on top.

SERVES: **4** | PREP TIME: **5 MINS** | COOKING TIME: **8 MINS**

Tofu and Pak Choi Stir-fry

2 tbsp coconut oil

350 g / 12 oz / 1 ½ cups firm tofu, cubed

2 cloves of garlic, crushed

1 tsp fresh root ginger, finely grated

1 red chilli (chili), finely chopped

100 g / 3 ½ oz / 1 cup mangetout

3 pak choi, sliced

2 tbsp soy sauce

3 tbsp orange juice

50 g / 1 ¾ oz / ½ cup raw cashew nuts, roughly chopped

1. Heat the oil in a large wok and brown the tofu on all sides. Transfer to a warm plate and set aside.
2. Add the garlic, ginger and chilli to the wok and stir-fry for 1 minute, then add the mangetout and pak choi and stir-fry for 2 minutes.
3. Pour in the soy and orange juice, then return the tofu to the wok and stir fry for 1 minute.
4. Sprinkle in the cashew nuts and serve immediately.

Salmon with Cucumber Salsa

4 portions salmon fillet

3 tbsp extra virgin olive oil

½ lemon, juiced

2 tsp runny honey

½ cucumber, seeds removed, flesh diced

8 radishes, diced

1 apple, cored and diced

1 celery stick, diced

1 small bunch flat leaf parsley, finely chopped

1. Heat the grill to its highest setting. Season the salmon with salt and pepper, then grill for 3 minutes on each side or until just cooked through.
2. Whisk the oil, lemon and honey together with a pinch of salt and pepper, then toss with the cucumber, radish, apple, celery and parsley.
3. Serve the salmon with the salsa spooned over the top.

Smashed Avocado on Toast

4 slices wholegrain bread

2 ripe avocados, halved and stoned

1 lime, juiced

2 spring onions (scallions), very finely chopped

tomato, cucumber or fried quail eggs to serve

flat leaf parsley to garnish

1. Toast the bread under a hot grill until crisp on both sides.
2. Meanwhile, scoop the avocado flesh into a bowl and mash roughly with a fork, incorporating the lime juice and spring onion as you go.
3. Season to taste with salt and pepper.
4. Spread the avocado onto the toast, add the toppings of your choice and garnish with parsley.

SERVES: 4 | PREP TIME: 10 MINS | COOKING TIME: 25 MINS

Roasted Broccoli Salad

1 head of broccoli, cut into florets
4 tbsp extra virgin olive oil
¼ tsp ground cumin
¼ tsp ground coriander
200 g / 7 oz / 1 cup canned chickpeas, rinsed and drained
100 g / 3 ½ oz / 3 cups baby leaf spinach
2 mild red chillies (chilies), sliced

FOR THE DRESSING
1 tsp tahini paste
1 tsp runny honey
1 tbsp lemon juice
1 clove of garlic, crushed
50 ml / 1 ¾ fl. oz / ¼ cup soya yogurt

1. Preheat the oven to 200°C (180°C fan) / 400F / gas 6.
2. Arrange the broccoli in a single layer in a large roasting tin. Drizzle it with half of the oil and sprinkle with salt, pepper and the ground spices. Roast the broccoli for 25 minutes, turning halfway through.
3. Meanwhile, make the dressing. Dissolve the tahini and honey in the lemon juice, then incorporate the garlic and yogurt. Season to taste with salt.
4. When the broccoli is ready, toss it with the chickpeas, spinach and chillies and divide between four bowls. Drizzle over the dressing and serve immediately.

SERVES: 6 | PREP TIME: 5 MINS | COOKING TIME: 40 MINS

Lentil and Vegetable Soup

3 tbsp extra virgin olive oil
1 onion, quartered and sliced
2 cloves of garlic, crushed
1 tsp ground coriander
1 tsp ground cumin
½ tsp smoked paprika
1 carrot, peeled and diced
¼ white cabbage, chopped
200 g / 7 oz / 1 cup red lentils
200 g / 7 oz / 1 cup green lentils
1.2 litres / 2 pint / 5 cups fresh vegetable stock
1 small handful flat-leaf parsley, chopped

1. Heat the oil in a large saucepan and fry the onion for 5 minutes. Add the garlic and fry for 2 minutes. Stir in the spices, then add the vegetables and lentils and stir well to coat.
2. Pour in the stock and cook over a high heat until it starts to boil.
3. Reduce the heat and simmer for 30 minutes or until the lentils are tender. Season to taste with salt and pepper.
4. Ladle the soup into warm bowls and sprinkle with parsley.

SERVES: **4** | PREP TIME: **10 MINS** | COOKING TIME: **35 MINS**

Couscous Bean Salad

200 g / 7 oz extra-firm tofu, in 1 piece

1 tbsp sea salt

300 g / 10 ½ oz / 1 ¾ cups couscous

400 g / 14 oz / 2 cups canned mixed beans, rinsed and drained

200 g / 7 oz / 1 cup canned sweetcorn, rinsed and drained

¼ broccoli, grated

50 g / 1 ¾ oz / ¼ cup sultanas

4 tbsp extra virgin olive oil

2 limes, juiced

1 tsp runny honey

300 g / 10 ½ oz / 2 cups edamame (soya) beans, defrosted if frozen

1 handful micro herbs

1. Sprinkle the tofu all over with salt, then sandwich it between two double layers of kitchen paper and weigh it down with a heavy wooden chopping board. Leave for 2 hours or preferably overnight.

2. Cook the couscous according to the packet instructions and leave to cool. Toss the couscous with the beans, sweetcorn, grated broccoli and sultanas.

3. Whisk the oil with the lime juice and honey and season to taste with salt and pepper. Stir half of the dressing into the salad.

4. Boil the edamame for 5 minutes or until tender, then plunge into iced water to cool. Drain well.

5. Crumble the salted tofu and toss with the edamame, micro herbs and the rest of the dressing. Serve with the bean and couscous salad.

Roasted Squash Salad

1 butternut squash, peeled, seeded and cut into fingers

3 tbsp extra virgin olive oil

1 tsp cumin seeds

4 plum tomatoes, quartered

100 g / 3 ½ oz / ¾ cup pecan nuts

½ lemon, zest finely grated

½ lime, zest finely grated

1 handful coriander (cilantro) leaves, chopped

FOR THE DRESSING

1 tsp tahini paste

1 tsp runny honey

1 tbsp lemon juice

1 tbsp lime juice

1 clove of garlic, crushed

50 ml / 1 ¾ fl. oz / ¼ cup soya yogurt

1. Preheat the oven to 200°C (180°C fan) / 400F / gas 6.
2. Arrange the squash in a single layer in a large roasting tin. Drizzle it with oil and sprinkle with salt, pepper and cumin seeds. Roast the squash for 40 minutes, turning it over and adding the tomatoes halfway through.
3. Meanwhile, make the dressing. Dissolve the tahini and honey in the lemon and lime juice, then incorporate the garlic and yogurt. Season to taste with salt.
4. When the squash is tender, divide it between four plates and scatter over the pecans, citrus zest and coriander. Drizzle with dressing and serve immediately.

Tomato Courgetti

4 small courgettes (zucchini)

2 avocados, peeled, stoned and sliced

225 g / 8 oz / 1 ½ cups cherry tomatoes, halved

½ red onion, sliced

2 tbsp flat-leaf parsley, chopped

FOR THE DRESSING

3 tbsp extra virgin olive oil

1 tbsp cider vinegar

1 tsp runny honey

1. Use a spiralizer to turn the courgettes into spaghetti-like ribbons.
2. Toss with the avocado, tomatoes, onion and parsley and divide between four bowls.
3. Make a simple dressing by shaking the oil, vinegar and honey together in a small jar. Season with salt and pepper and serve with the salads.

SERVES: **4-6** | PREP TIME: **20 MINS** | COOKING TIME: **25 MINS**

Cabbage Stew with Chorizo

1 tsp rapeseed oil
100 g / 3 ½ oz chorizo, sliced
1 onion, diced
2 garlic cloves, chopped
1 tsp tomato puree
500 g / 1 lb 2 oz white cabbage, shredded
500 g / 1 lb 2 oz carrots, cut into small batons
1 tsp wholegrain mustard
200 ml / 7 fl. oz / 1 cup vegetable stock
200 g / 7 oz sauerkraut
sea salt and black pepper
28 g flat leaf parsley, chopped

1. In a large casserole dish, heat the oil over a medium heat. Add the chorizo and fry for 5 minutes turning occasionally. Remove the chorizo with a slotted spoon and set aside.
2. Add the onions to the pan and cook for 5 minutes until soft and translucent, then add the garlic. Fry for a further minute before adding the tomato puree and continuing to cook for 30 seconds.
3. Add the shredded cabbage and carrots to the pan and cook for 10 minutes, stirring regularly. Return the chorizo to the pan before adding the mustard, stock and sauerkraut. Cook for a further 10 minutes until tender. Season to taste with salt and black pepper and stir through the parsley before serving.

Fresh Pea Soup

2 tbsp extra virgin olive oil
1 leek, chopped
2 cloves of garlic, crushed
1 large potato, peeled and diced
1 litre / 1 pint 14 fl. oz / 4 cups fresh
    vegetable stock
200 g / 7 oz / 1 ⅓ cups fresh peas,
    podded weight
50 g / 1 ¾ oz / 1 ½ cups pea shoots

1. Heat the oil in a saucepan and fry the leeks for 8 minutes or until softened.
2. Add the garlic and potato to the pan and cook for 2 more minutes, then pour
   in the stock.
3. Simmer for 15 minutes, then stir in three quarters of the peas and cook for 3 minutes.
4. Transfer the soup to a liquidizer with half of the pea shoots and blend until smooth.
   Season to taste with salt and black pepper.
5. Pour the soup into four bowls and garnish with the rest of the peas and pea shoots.

Lentils with Root Vegetables

4 large carrots, sliced
1 butternut squash, peeled, deseeded
    and cubed
2 tsp olive oil
1 medium onion, diced
1 garlic glove, finely chopped
1 red chilli (chili), finely chopped
1 tbsp tomato puree
250 g / 8 ½ oz / 1 ¼ cups lentils
1 pinch of cayenne
500 ml / 17 fl. oz / 2 cups vegetable stock
1 handful of chopped parsley
sea salt and freshly ground black pepper

1. Preheat the oven to 230°C (210°C fan) / 450F / gas 8.
2. Place the carrot and butternut squash onto a baking tray and drizzle with oil.
   Toss to coat the vegetables and season before placing into the oven for
   20 minutes. Remove from the oven and set aside for later.
3. In a casserole dish, heat the oil and fry the onion until translucent on a medium.
   Add the garlic and chilli and fry for a further 2 minutes before adding the tomato
   puree and cayenne. Fry for a further minute before stirring in the lentils and
   adding the vegetable stock. Cover and simmer for 40 minutes or until the lentils
   are fully cooked.
4. Once the lentils are cooked, add the roasted vegetables back into the pan to warm.
   Add the chopped parsley, season with salt and black pepper, then serve.

SERVES: **4** | PREP TIME: **10 MINS** | COOKING TIME: **20 MINS**

Spicy Salad Wraps

150 g / 5 ½ oz / 1 cup ripe
   tomatoes, chopped

1 tbsp coconut sugar

1 tbsp cider vinegar

1 tsp smoked paprika

100 ml / 3 ½ fl. oz / ½ cup soya yogurt

2 gherkins, finely chopped

1 spring onion (scallion), finely chopped

½ tbsp capers, finely chopped

4 wholegrain or gluten-free tortillas

75 g / 2 ½ oz / 2 ¼ cups rocket (arugula)

12 cherry tomatoes, halved

200 g / 7 oz / 1 cup canned
   sweetcorn, drained

4 slices red pepper

4 green chillies (chilies), sliced

1. To make the ketchup, put the
   tomatoes in a saucepan with the
   sugar, vinegar and paprika.

2. Cook, covered, until the mixture
   starts to boil, then reduce the
   heat and simmer uncovered for
   15 minutes. Blend until smooth and
   leave to cool.

3. To make the yogurt dressing, combine
   the yogurt with the gherkins, spring
   onion and capers and set aside.

4. Lay out the tortillas and top with
   rocket, tomatoes, sweetcorn, pepper
   and chillies. Serve with the ketchup
   and yogurt dressing for drizzling over
   or dipping into.

King Prawn Courgetti

2 large courgettes or 300g / 10.5 oz
  pre-made courgetti
2 tsp olive oil
1 banana shallot, finely diced
1 garlic clove, finely sliced
1 green chilli, de-seeded and finely chopped
200 g / 7 oz raw king prawns, peeled
1 lemon, zest and juice
1 handful of fresh basil, finely chopped
1 handful of flat leaf parsley, finely chopped

1. Using a spiralizer, cut the courgettes into thin ribbons of courgetti. Alternatively, if you do not have a spiralizer, cut lengthways into ribbons and then again into thin strips. Either steam or boil for 2-3 minutes until al dente, then drain and set aside but keep warm.
2. Heat the olive oil in a large frying pan over a medium heat and add the shallots. Cook for 3 minutes until softened before adding the garlic, chilli and lemon zest and cooking for a further minute.
3. Add the prawns and half the lemon juice and cook for around 5 minutes until the prawns are slightly firm and pink.
4. Toss the remaining lemon juice and herbs through the courgetti, season and divide between two bowls before topping with the cooked prawns.

Winter Salad with Kale

2 large sweet potatoes (yams), cut into bite
  sized chunks
1 tsp cayenne
1 tsp smoked paprika
3 tsp olive oil
500 g / 1 lb 2 oz curly kale, stems removed
  and sliced
2 garlic cloves, finely sliced
1 red chilli (chili), de-seeded and
  finely chopped
200 g / 7 oz heirloom cherry
  tomotoes, halved
25 g / ½ cup pumpkin seeds
1 tsp sesame seeds
2 large avocados, sliced

1. Preheat the oven to 200°C (180°C fan) / 400F / gas 6 and combine the sweet potato, cayenne, paprika and 2 teaspoons of the olive oil in a bowl. Toss together to coat the potato with spices before spreading evenly on a baking tray.
2. Place in the oven and cook for 20-25 minutes until caramelized.
3. While the potato is cooking, bring a large pan of salted water to the boil and cook the kale for 2-3 minutes, then drain well.
4. Heat the remaining oil on a medium heat in a large sauté pan and add the chilli and garlic. Fry for 1 minute until fragrant. Add the kale and cook for 8-10 minutes until tender.
5. To serve, evenly distribute the kale between four bowls and top with the sweet potato, tomatoes, seeds and sliced avocado.

Stir-fried Mushroom and Mange Tout

200 g / 7 oz chestnut mushrooms, sliced

200 g / 7 oz mange tout, trimmed

2 tsp coconut oil

1 garlic clove, crushed

20 g fresh ginger, minced

1 tsp Chinese five-spice powder

1 tsp raw honey

20 ml low sodium soy sauce

1 tsp cornflour (corn starch)

1 handful of coriander (cilantro), finely chopped inc. stems

1 tsp sesame seeds

1. Heat a wok or large frying pan on a high heat and add the coconut oil. Once the oil is smoking add the mushrooms and mange tout and stir-fry for 2 to 3 minutes until tender.
2. Add the garlic and ginger and continue to stir-fry for 1 minute, then remove from the wok and set aside.
3. In a small bowl, combine the Chinese five-spice, honey, soy and corn flour to create a paste. Add this to the hot wok and cook for 15 seconds to thicken before adding the vegetables to the wok again. Toss to coat and add the coriander and sesame seeds.
4. Serve immediately with brown rice.

Raw Kale Salad

TO MAKE THE VINAIGRETTE
1 tbsp Dijon mustard
60 ml / 2 fl. oz / ¼ cup apple cider vinegar
1 lemon, juiced
1 tbsp raw organic honey
100 ml / 3 fl. oz / ½ cup extra virgin
  olive oil

TO MAKE THE SALAD
200 g / 7 oz kale
1 red onion, sliced
2 large carrots, cut into batons
1 large avocado, sliced
100g / 3 ½ oz radish, thinly sliced
100g / 3 ½ oz cooked beetroot, cut
  into batons
2 Braeburn apples, cored and sliced
1 tsp black sesame seeds
1 tsp chia seeds

1. To make the vinaigrette, combine the first 5 ingredients in a jar before sealing and shaking well. Season to taste, adding more honey, if desired. Leave to combine for 30 minutes before using. This will keep in the fridge for up to one week.
2. Prepare the kale by removing the tough stems and cutting it into bite-sized pieces. Place it into a bowl, add some salt and squeeze the leaves to soften them.
3. Add the remaining salad ingredients to the kale except for the seeds. Pour over the vinaigrette and toss the salad to coat the leaves. Sprinkle over the seeds and serve.

Mixed Berry Summer Salad

300 g / 10.5 oz crispy leaf salad (such as
  Friseé or Radiccio), washed
100 g / 3.5 oz sorrel leaves, washed
2 large avocado, sliced
200 g / 7 oz / ¾ cup mixed berries
  (strawberries, blackberries,
  raspberries, blueberries)
40 g cress
1 tbsp Dijon mustard
1 tbsp manuka honey
1 garlic glove, crushed
2 tbsp cider vinegar
6 tbsp avocado oil

1. Arrange the salad leaves on plates and top with the avocado, blackberries, raspberries and blueberries.
2. Remove any stalks and slice the strawberries. Place the sliced strawberries and cress in the centre of the salad.
3. Place the mustard, honey, garlic and vinegar in a food processor and blitz together. Gradually pour in the avocado oil whilst continuing to blend.
4. Drizzle the dressing over the salad and serve.

SERVES: **4-6** | PREP TIME: **45 MINS**

Hearty Pasta Casserole

500 g / 1 lb 2 oz gluten-free pasta
1 tbsp olive oil
200 g / 7 oz pancetta
1 white onion, finely chopped
2 large carrots, diced
3 garlic gloves, finely chopped
2 large tomatoes, chopped
1 tbsp brown rice flour
1 tbsp Dijon mustard
500 ml / 17 fl. oz / 2 cups milk
400 g / 14 oz cannellini beans, drained
2 sprigs of thyme, leaves only
120 g / 4 oz cavolo nero, chopped
salt and freshly ground black pepper

1. Cook the pasta for 10 minutes or according to packet instructions until cooked al dente. Drain and set aside.
2. Heat the oil in a casserole or large heavy bottomed pan and add the pancetta. Fry for 4-5 minutes until slightly crisp before adding the onion and carrot. Continue to fry for a further 5 minutes or until the onion has slightly browned before adding the garlic and tomato and fry for a further minute.
3. Sprinkle over the flour stirring constantly for around a minute before adding the mustard followed by half of the milk and continuing to stir. Gradually add the rest of the milk, stirring after each addition until you have a thick sauce. Add the beans and warm through for around 10 minutes. Then add the thyme leaves.
4. In a pan of salted boiling water, cook the cavolo nero for 2 minutes and drain. When ready to serve, add the cavolo nero to the pasta and season with salt and freshly ground black pepper.

Raw Vegetable Salad

3 large carrots, peeled
3 large courgettes (zucchini)
1 cucumber, sliced
200 g / 7 oz radish, thinly sliced
1 handful chopped parsley
6 tsp extra virgin olive oil
juice of 2 lemons
salt and freshly ground black pepper

1. Using a mandolin or vegetable peeler, cut the carrot and courgette lengthways into thin ribbons. Combine with the cucumber, radish and parsley in a bowl.
2. Mix the oil and lemon juice in a small jar and shake with the lid on the jar. Pour this dressing over the vegetables and toss to combine, seasoning with salt and pepper to taste.
3. Place into a large serving bowl.
4. This salad is perfect served with barbecued meats or steamed fish.

Courgetti with Mushrooms

2 large courgettes (zucchini) or 300g pre-made courgetti
200 g / 7 oz closed cup chestnut mushrooms, chopped
1 garlic clove, minced
2 tsp olive oil
salt and freshly ground black pepper
fresh basil to garnish

1. Using a spiralizer, cut the courgettes into thin ribbons known as courgetti. Alternatively, if you do not have a spiralizer, cut lengthways into thin ribbons and then again into thin strips.
2. Add the courgetti to a pan of salted boiling water and cook for 2 minutes until tender. Drain well and set aside.
3. Heat the oil in a frying pan over a medium heat and sauté the mushrooms with the garlic until softened. Add the courgetti and stir through to heat before seasoning with salt and pepper.
4. Divide equally between two plates and garnish with fresh basil and drizzle with olive oil.

SERVES: **2** | PREP TIME: **15 MINS** | MARINATE: **1 HOUR** | COOKING TIME: **15 MINS**

Chicken and Mushroom Salad

2 chicken breasts

1 lemon, juiced

2 tsp olive oil

2 cloves of garlic, unpeeled and lightly crushed

3 sprigs of fresh thyme

100 g / 3 ½ oz closed cup mushrooms, halved

1 large avocado, sliced

100 g / 3 ½ oz vine cherry tomatoes

80 g / 3 oz baby leaf spinach and rocket salad

balsamic vinegar glaze to finish

salt and freshly ground black pepper

1. Place the chicken breasts between two pieces of cling film and lightly flatten by hitting with a rolling pin. Combine the chicken with the lemon juice, olive oil, garlic and thyme in a bowl and cover. Leave to marinade in the refrigerator for at least 1 hour.

2. Remove chicken from the refrigerator 20 minutes before cooking.

3. Heat a griddle pan to a medium-high heat and cook the chicken for around 5 minutes on each side. Once the chicken is fully cooked, remove to rest and cook the mushrooms on the griddle pan until lightly charred.

4. To serve, arrange the salad leaves on plates scattering over the avocado, cherry tomatoes and mushrooms. Slice the chicken into strips and drizzle over the balsamic glaze. Season with salt and pepper and serve with crusty bread and extra virgin oil.

Mushroom and Tofu Galettes

200 g / 7 oz extra-firm tofu, in 1 piece
1 tbsp sea salt
3 tbsp extra virgin olive oil
150 g / 5 ½ oz / 2 cups mushrooms, sliced
1 tbsp fresh thyme leaves
2 cloves of garlic, crushed
a few chives to garnish

FOR THE GALETTE BATTER
75 g / 2 ½ oz / ½ cup buckwheat flour
1 large egg
150 ml / 5 ½ fl. oz / ⅔ cup soya
    or almond milk
1 tbsp coconut oil, melted, plus extra for frying

1. Sprinkle the tofu all over with salt, then sandwich it between two double layers of kitchen paper and weigh it down with a heavy wooden chopping board. Leave for 2 hours or preferably overnight.
2. To make the galette batter, put all of the ingredients in a liquidizer and blend until smooth. Rest the batter in the fridge for at least 2 hours.
3. Grease a crêpe pan with coconut oil and set it over a medium heat. Add a ladle of batter and swirl to coat the base of the pan. Cook for 1–2 minutes on each side then repeat with the rest of the batter to form four galettes. Keep warm.
4. Heat the olive oil in a sauté pan and fry the mushrooms and thyme with a pinch of salt for 10 minutes. Add the garlic and sauté for 2 minutes.
5. Divide the mushrooms between the galettes and crumble over the salted tofu. Garnish with chives and fold in the edges. Delicious served with spinach and cherry tomatoes.

Quinoa and Mackerel Salad

150 g / 5 ½ oz / ¾ cup black quinoa
3 tbsp extra virgin olive oil
1 lemon, juiced and zest finely grated
½ tsp chilli (chili) flakes
1 clove of garlic, crushed
2 tsp runny honey
2 tbsp baby capers
150 g / 5 ½ oz / 4 ½ cups baby chard leaves
2 smoked mackerel fillets, skinned, boned
    and flaked

1. Put the quinoa in a saucepan with 350 ml water. Cover and simmer gently for 10 minutes, then leave to stand off the heat for a further 15 minutes without lifting the lid.
2. Whisk the olive oil, lemon juice and zest, chilli flakes, garlic, honey and capers in a bowl and season to taste with salt and pepper.
3. Stir the quinoa into the dressing and leave to cool to room temperature.
4. Toss the quinoa with the baby chard leaves and flaked smoked mackerel, then divide between four plates and serve immediately.

Spinach and Strawberry Salad

200 g / 7 oz extra-firm tofu, in 1 piece
1 tbsp sea salt
150 g / 5 ½ oz / 4 ½ cups baby leaf spinach
150 g / 5 ½ oz / 1 cup strawberries, sliced
30 g / ½ cup almonds, roughly chopped
3 tbsp extra virgin olive oil
2 tbsp balsamic vinegar
1 tsp runny honey
1 clove of garlic, crushed

1. Sprinkle the tofu all over with the salt, then sandwich it between two double layers of kitchen paper and weigh it down with a heavy wooden chopping board. Leave for 2 hours or preferably overnight.
2. Divide the spinach between four bowls and scatter over the strawberries and almonds.
3. Whisk the oil, vinegar, honey and garlic together with a pinch of salt and drizzle over the salad.
4. Crumble the salted tofu over the salad and add plenty of freshly ground black pepper.

Spiced Grilled Salmon

4 salmon steaks, halved and boned
1 lime, sliced
2 tsp chilli (chili) flakes

FOR THE SPICE PASTE
2 cloves of garlic, chopped
1 tbsp fresh root ginger, chopped
30 g / 1 cup Thai basil, leaves only, plus extra to garnish
30 g coriander (cilantro), leaves only
2 green chillies (chilies), chopped
2 tbsp cashew nuts
1 lime, zest finely grated
3 tbsp extra virgin olive oil

1. Soak eight wooden skewers in water for 20 minutes before using to stop them from burning.
2. To make the spice paste, put all of the ingredients in a food processor and blend until smooth.
3. Thread the salmon onto the skewers and brush them all over with the paste. Any unused paste can be served in a small bowl alongside for dipping.
4. Arrange the salmon skewers and lime slices on a grill tray and cook under a very hot grill for 3 minutes on each side or until golden brown.
5. Serve the salmon with a small bowl of chilli flakes for sprinkling over at the table.

SERVES: 4 | PREP TIME: 15 MINS

Greek Couscous Salad

250 g / 9 oz / 1 ½ cups couscous

400 ml / 13 ½ fl. oz / 1 ½ cups chicken or vegetable stock

a handful of flat leaf parsley, finely chopped

a handful of fresh mint, finely chopped

a handful of fresh basil, finely chopped

½ red onion, finely sliced

1 cucumber, finely sliced

1 lemon, zested and juiced

20 g Kalamata olives, finely diced

100 g / 3 ½ oz feta cheese, cubed

60 ml / 2 fl. oz / ¼ cup extra virgin olive oil

1 tsp chilli (chili) flakes

1 tsp agave syrup

100 g / 3 ½ oz / ¾ cup walnut halves

1. Place the couscous in a bowl and pour in the hot stock. Stir once, cover with a plate or cling film and leave for approximately 5 minutes or until the liquid has been absorbed. Fluff with a fork to separate the grains before stirring through the chopped herbs, onion, cucumber, lemon zest, olives and feta cheese.

2. Place the lemon juice, oil, chilli flakes and honey into a small jar and shake well to combine. Pour over the couscous salad and mix well to combine, season to taste.

3. Sprinkle over the walnut pieces before serving.

SERVES: 4 | PREP TIME: 20 MINS | COOKING: 3 HOURS 30 MINS | REST: 15 MINS

Pot Roast Lamb with Vegetables

1 kg / 2.2 lb shoulder of organic free-range lamb, boned and rolled

3 tsp rapeseed oil

sea salt and freshly ground black pepper

a handful of fresh rosemary, chopped

1 bulb of garlic, cloves removed unpeeled lightly crushed

250 g / 9 oz carrots, roughly chopped

1 large onion, roughly chopped

250 g / 9 oz baby potatoes, chopped

200 g / 7 oz Brussels sprouts, outer leaves removed

200 g / 7 oz cherry tomatoes

1. Preheat the oven to 180°C (160°C fan) / 350F / gas 4.
2. Season the lamb with salt and pepper, 2 teaspoons of oil and half the rosemary and rub all over getting into the folds and edges, then set aside.
3. In a large casserole dish, combine the remaining rosemary, oil, garlic, carrots, onion, potatoes and sprouts. Sit the lamb on top of the vegetables and cover with the lid, or foil, and roast in the oven for 3 hours.
4. Remove the lid or foil, add the chopped tomatoes and roast for a further 30 minutes. Remove from the oven and place the meat on a chopping board, cover with foil and allow to rest for 15 minutes.
5. While the meat is resting, keep the vegetables warm in the oven with the heat off.
6. Once the meat has rested, either serve separately on a chopping board or atop the vegetables.

SERVES: 12 | PREP TIME: 15 MINS | CHILLING TIME: 1 HOUR

Chicken Summer Rolls

8 rice paper wrappers
8 soft lettuce leaves
2 cold roast chicken breasts, sliced
1 red pepper, deseeded and sliced
1 red onion, halved and sliced
¼ cucumber, julienned
75 g / 2 ½ oz / 2 ¼ cups pea shoots

FOR THE DIPPING SAUCE
2 tbsp caster sugar
2 limes, juiced
2 tbsp fish sauce
1 red chilli (chili), sliced
½ garlic clove, finely chopped

1. First make the dipping sauce.
   Stir the sugar into the lime juice until it dissolves, then stir in the fish sauce, chilli and garlic. Taste the dressing and adjust the levels of sweet, sour and salty, then set aside to infuse.

2. Dip the first rice paper wrapper in a bowl of cold water, then lay it out on a clean chopping board. Lay a lettuce leaf on top and add some chicken, pepper, onion, cucumber and pea shoots.

3. Fold over the bottom edge of the wrapper, then roll it up to enclose the filling, leaving the top edge open.

4. Repeat with the rest of the ingredients to form eight rolls, then serve immediately with the dipping sauce.

Turkey Kebabs

600 g / 20 oz turkey breast, cut into 2 cm (1 in) cubes

2 courgettes (zucchini), sliced

1 red onion, cut into wedges

2 red peppers, cut into wedges

2 tsp olive oil

1 lemon, juiced

sea salt and black pepper

1. Soak the bamboo skewers in water for at least 10 minutes before preparing.
2. Ensure that the vegetable pieces are cut into evenly sized pieces so that they cook evenly. Add to the skewers alternating each of the vegetables and the turkey.
3. Mix the oil with the lemon juice and brush over the kebabs before seasoning well with salt and black pepper.
4. Cook on a barbecue, griddle or under the grill for approximately 15-20 minutes until the chicken has started to caramelise and the vegetables have started to char at the edges.
5. Serve with a fresh salad and a yogurt dip.

Healthy Organic Salad

1 sweet potato (yam), cubed

1 tsp olive oil

50 g / 1 ¾ oz farro

200 g / 7 oz leafy green salad (such as Cos, curly leaf lettuce or Romaine)

200 g / 7 oz roasted red peppers, sliced

60 ml / 2 fl. oz rapeseed oil

30 ml / 1 fl. oz balsamic vinegar

1 avocado, sliced

30 g lamb's lettuce

1. Preheat the oven to 200°C (180°C fan) / 400F / gas 6.
2. Coat the cubed sweet potato with the oil and season before roasting in the oven for 15-20 minutes until tender. Remove and set aside.
3. While the sweet potato is cooking, add the farro to a pan of boiling water and cook for 10 minutes until tender. Drain well and season.
4. Roughly chop the salad leaves and place in a large bowl with the peppers. Whisk together the oil and vinegar and season before pouring over the salad and tossing to coat the leaves.
5. Divide the leaves among serving plates or bowls and arrange the sweet potato and cooled farro on the leaves. Top with the sliced avocado and finish with the lamb's lettuce. Season and drizzle a little oil over the top to finish.

SERVES: **4** | PREP TIME: **15 MINS** | COOKING TIME: **20 MINS**

Chicken Kebabs and Cucumber Salad

600 g / 20 oz chicken breast, diced
4 tsp olive oil
2 lemons, juiced
a handful of dill, finely chopped
sea salt and freshly ground black pepper
1 shallot, finely sliced
1 tsp white wine vinegar
1 tsp Dijon mustard
a pinch of chilli (chili) flakes
a handful of flat leaf parsley, chopped
a few fresh mint leaves, chopped
1 cucumber, finely sliced

1. In a large bowl, mix the chicken, half the oil, half the lemon juice and dill.
   Season with salt and pepper, then cover and set aside until ready to cook.
2. Soak the bamboo skewers in water for at least 10 minutes before sliding on the
   chicken pieces. Cook on a barbecue, griddle or under the grill for approximately
   15-20 minutes until the chicken has started to caramelise and is fully cooked.
3. To prepare the cucumber salad, combine the remaining oil and lemon juice with
   the shallot, vinegar, mustard, chilli and herbs. Mix well and season before leaving
   for 5 minutes to combine and create a dressing.
4. When ready to serve, pour the dressing over the cucumber and mix to coat.
5. Serve the cucumber salad with chicken kebabs.

SERVES: **4-6** | PREP TIME: **15 MINS** | COOKING TIME: **1 HOUR**

Beetroot and Feta salad

500 g / 1 lb 2 oz beetroot
125 ml / 4 fl. oz / ½ cup cider vinegar
400 ml / 13 ½ fl. oz / 1 ½ cups water
1 bay leaf
1 tsp black peppercorns
1 star anise
300 g / 10 ½ oz / 1 ½ cups quinoa
70 g / 2 ½ oz ruby chard
200 g / 7 oz feta cheese
30 g pumpkin seeds
30 ml balsamic vinegar
1 tsp olive oil
1 tsp date syrup
1 tsp Dijon mustard
1 garlic clove, crushed
sea salt and black pepper

1. Place the whole beetroot in a large saucepan with the vinegar, water, bay leaf, peppercorns and star anise and bring to a boil. Lower the heat to a simmer, cover and cook for around 45 minutes until tender. Drain and leave to cool before peeling and chopping into chunks.

2. Cook the quinoa whilst the beetroot is cooling as per the packet instructions. Drain well and spread on a baking tray to steam dry.

3. Place the quinoa on a plate and top with the chard leaves before scattering the crumbled feta, cooked beetroot and pumpkin seeds.

4. Whisk together the balsamic, oil, syrup, mustard and garlic and season to taste. Drizzle over the top of the salad and serve.

Desserts

Chocolate Raspberry Tarts

FOR THE CRUST

250 g / 9 oz / 1 ⅔ cups
  blanched almonds

25 g pure cacao powder

2 tbsp coconut flour

50 ml / 1 ¾ fl. oz / ¼ cup maple syrup

3 tbsp coconut oil, melted

FOR THE FILLING

150 g / 5 oz / 1 cup raspberries

225 ml / 8 fl. oz / ¾ cup canned
  coconut milk

300 g / 10 ½ oz / 2 cups dark chocolate
  (min. 85 per cent cocoa solids),
  finely chopped

2 tbsp coconut oil

coconut flour for sprinkling

1. Put the almonds, cacao and coconut flour in a food processor and process until finely ground. Add the maple syrup and coconut oil and pulse until it forms a dough. Press the dough into the base and sides of eight small tart moulds.

2. Reserve eight raspberries and mash the rest with a fork. Spoon a little into each mould.

3. Put the coconut milk in a small saucepan with a pinch of salt and heat it gently. Meanwhile, put the chocolate and coconut oil in a mixing bowl.

4. When the coconut milk starts to simmer, pour it over the chocolate in the bowl. Leave it to stand for 30 seconds, then stir gently until it forms a homogenous smooth ganache.

5. Divide the ganache between the moulds then chill for 3 hours or until set.

6. Garnish each tart with a raspberry and a sprinkle of coconut flour.

SERVES: 6 | PREP TIME: 10 MINS | FREEZING TIME: 3-4 HOURS

Tropical Fruit Sorbet

2 ripe mangoes, peeled, stoned and chopped
2 ripe papaya, peeled, seeded and chopped
2 passion fruit, pulp sieved and seeds discarded
1 banana, peeled and chopped
100 ml / 3 ½ fl. oz / ½ cup pure pineapple juice
50 g / 1 ¾ oz / ¼ cup coconut sugar
mint sprigs or lemon balm to garnish

1. Put all of the ingredients, except the herbs, in a liquidizer and blend until very smooth.
2. Churn in an ice cream maker, according to the manufacturer's instructions, then freeze for 2 hours.
3. Alternatively, scrape the mixture into a plastic box with a lid and freeze for 2 hours. Scrape the semi-frozen mixture into a food processor and blend until smooth, then return it to the box and freeze for 1 hour. Whizz the mixture in the food processor again, then freeze until firm.
4. Scoop the sorbet into glasses and garnish with mint or lemon balm.

Black Bean Brownies

50 g / 1 ¾ oz / ½ cup rolled porridge oats

2 tbsp pure cacao powder

1 tsp baking powder

400 g / 14 oz / 2 cups canned black beans,
   drained and rinsed

100 ml / 3 ½ fl. oz / ½ cup maple syrup

50 ml / 1 ¾ oz / ¼ cup coconut oil, melted

1 vanilla pod, seeds only

100 g / 3 ½ oz / ⅔ cup dark chocolate
   (min. 85 per cent cocoa solids),
   finely chopped

1. Preheat the oven to 180°C (160°C fan) / 350F / gas 4 and oil and line a 20 cm (8 in) square cake tin with greaseproof paper.
2. Put the oats, cacao and baking powder in a food processor and blitz to a powder. Add the black beans, maple syrup, coconut oil and vanilla and blend again until very smooth.
3. Fold in the chopped chocolate, then scrape the mixture into the tin and level the top.
4. Bake for 20 minutes or until the outside is set, but the centre is still quite soft.
5. Leave the brownie to cool completely before cutting and serving.

Blueberry Crumbles

350 g / 12 ½ oz / 2 ⅓ cups blueberries

2 tbsp maple syrup

75 g / 2 ½ oz / ⅓ cup coconut oil

75 g / 2 ½ oz / ½ cup buckwheat flour

25 g / ¼ cup rolled buckwheat flakes

25 g / ¼ cup ground almonds

40 g / ¼ cup coconut sugar

lemon balm to garnish

1. Preheat the oven to 180°C (160°C fan) / 350F / gas 4.
2. Reserve a few of the berries for decoration, then mix the rest with the maple syrup and divide them between six ramekin dishes.
3. Rub the coconut oil into the buckwheat flour then stir in the buckwheat flakes, ground almonds and coconut sugar.
4. Crumble the mixture over the blueberries then bake for 25 minutes or until the topping is brown and crisp.
5. Garnish with the reserved berries and lemon balm just before serving.

SERVES: **6** | PREP TIME: **45 MINS** | FREEZING TIME: **4 HOURS**

Raw Berry Cheesecake

150 g / 5 oz / 1 cup mixed frozen berries, defrosted
2 tbsp coconut sugar
250 g / 9 oz / 1 ½ cups medjool dates, stoned
225 g / 8 oz / 2 ¼ cups ground almonds
250 g / 9 oz / 1 ⅔ cups raw cashew nuts, soaked overnight
400 ml / 14 fl. oz / 2 cup canned coconut milk, chilled unopened
1 ½ lemons, juiced and zest finely grated
75 ml / 2 ½ fl. oz / ⅓ cup maple syrup
50 ml 1 ¾ oz / ¼ cup runny honey
¼ tsp nutmeg, freshly grated

1. Mix the berries with the coconut sugar and leave to macerate for 20 minutes.
2. Soak the dates in warm water for 10 minutes, then drain and blend to a smooth paste in a food processor. Add the ground almonds and pulse until it forms a dough. Line a 20 cm (8 in) round spring-form cake tin with clingfilm, then press the mixture into the base.
3. Drain the cashews and put them in the food processor. Open the can of coconut milk upside down and discard the thin watery layer. Scoop the thick creamy layer into the food processor and add the lemon juice, zest and maple syrup.
4. Blend until very smooth, pausing to scrape down the sides occasionally.
5. Spoon half of the macerated berries over the cheesecake base and top with the cashew mixture. Cover with clingfilm and freeze for at least 4 hours.
6. Remove from the freezer 20 minutes before serving. Unmould the cheesecake and cut into wedges. Mix the honey with the nutmeg and drizzle over the top, then serve with the rest of the berries on the side.

SERVES: **9** | PREP TIME: **45 MINS**

Chocolate, Coconut and Strawberry Slice

FOR THE BASE
150 g / 5 ½ oz / 1 cup medjool dates, stoned
1 tbsp coconut oil, melted
75 g / 2 ½ oz / ¾ cup desiccated coconut
75 g / 2 ½ oz / ¾ cup gluten-free porridge oats

FOR THE TOPPING
150 g / 5 ½ oz / 1 ½ cups desiccated coconut
100 g / 3 ½ oz / 1 cup ground almonds
4 limes, juiced
60 ml / 2 fl. oz / ¼ cup coconut oil, melted
60 ml / 2 fl. oz / ¼ cup runny honey
100 g / 3 ½ oz / ⅔ cup dark chocolate (min. 70 per cent cocoa solids), chopped
100 g / 3 ½ oz / ⅔ cup wild strawberries

1. Soak the dates in warm water for 10 minutes, then drain and blend to a smooth paste in a food processor with the coconut oil. Add the coconut and oats and blend again to form a paste.
2. Line a 23 cm (9 in) square cake tin with greaseproof paper then press the mixture into the base.
3. To make the topping, put the coconut, almonds, lime juice, coconut oil and honey in the food processor and blend to form a smooth soft paste. Scrape the mixture on top of the base and level with a palate knife. Chill for 30 minutes.
4. Melt the chocolate in a microwave or bain-marie. Drizzle the chocolate all over the topping, then scatter over the strawberries.
5. Cut into nine squares and serve immediately or store in the fridge for later.

MAKES: **6** | PREP TIME: **15 MINS** | FREEZING TIME: **4 HOURS**

Peach Melba
Ice Lollies

4 very ripe peaches, peeled,quartered
and stoned
350 g / 12 oz / 2 ⅓ cups raspberries

1. Put the peaches in a liquidizer and blend until smooth. Pour the mixture into a jug and set aside.
2. Put the raspberries in the liquidizer and blend, then pass the mixture through a sieve set over a jug to remove the seeds.
3. Divide the raspberry puree between six ice lolly moulds, then fill to the top with peach puree.
4. Insert sticks and cover according to the manufacturer's instructions. Freeze for at least 4 hours before unmoulding and serving.

SERVES: 2 | PREP TIME: 15 MINS

Citrus Salad

1 grapefruit

1 orange

2 blood oranges

1 handful of chopped mint leaves

1 pomegranate, seeds only

1 tsp raw organic honey

2 tsp extra virgin olive oil

a pinch of sea salt

1. To prepare the fruit, slice across the top and bottom of each before slicing off the peel, leaving as little of the white pith as possible. Slice into wheels, removing any pips, and arrange onto a plate.

2. Garnish the fruit with the chopped mint and pomegranate seeds.

3. Combine the honey and olive oil and drizzle over the salad before seasoning with sea salt.

MAKES: **8** | PREP TIME: **45 MINS** | FREEZING TIME: **4 HOURS**

Individual Strawberry Tortes

FOR THE BASE

150 g / 5 ½ oz / 1 cup medjool
dates, stoned
1 tbsp coconut oil, melted
75 g / 2 ½ oz / ¾ cup desiccated coconut
75 g / 2 ½ oz / ¾ cup gluten-free
porridge oats

FOR THE TOPPING

250 g / 9 oz / 1 ⅔ cups raw cashew nuts,
soaked overnight
400 ml / 14 fl. oz / 2 cup canned coconut
milk, chilled unopened
1 ½ lemons, juiced and zest finely grated
75 ml / 2 ½ fl. oz / ⅓ cup maple syrup
150 g / 5 ½ oz / 1 cup wild strawberries

1. Soak the dates in warm water for 10 minutes, then drain and blend to a smooth
   paste in a food processor with the coconut oil. Add the coconut and oats and
   blend again to form a paste.
2. Press the mixture into eight individual loose bottomed torte moulds.
3. Drain the cashews and put them in the food processor. Open the can of coconut
   milk upside down and discard the thin watery layer. Scoop the thick creamy layer
   into the food processor and add the lemon juice, zest and maple syrup.
4. Blend until very smooth, pausing to scrape down the sides occasionally.
   Pour 100 g of the mixture into a bowl and set aside in the fridge. Divide the rest
   of the mixture between the torte moulds and level the tops. Cover with clingfilm
   and freeze for at least 4 hours.
5. Remove the tortes from the freezer 20 minutes before serving. Put the reserved
   cashew mixture in the food processor with half of the strawberries and blend
   until smooth.
6. Unmould the tortes and spoon over the strawberry topping. Scatter with the rest
   of the strawberries and serve immediately.

Oat and Coconut Loaf Cake

150 g / 5 ½ oz / 1 cup gluten-free plain (all-purpose) flour

125 g / 4 ½ oz / 1 ¼ cups rolled porridge oats

50 g / 1 ¾ oz / ½ cup desiccated or flaked coconut

1 tsp bicarbonate of (baking) soda

3 very ripe bananas

50 ml / 1 ¾ fl. oz / ¼ cup coconut milk

50 ml / 1 ¾ fl. oz / ¼ cup coconut oil, melted

75 ml / 2 ½ fl. oz / ⅓ cup runny honey

250 g / 9 oz / 1 ½ cup cooked quinoa

coconut butter to serve

1. Preheat the oven to 180°C (160°C fan) / 350F / gas 4 and oil and line a large loaf tin with greaseproof paper.
2. Mix together the flour, oats, coconut and baking soda in a large mixing bowl and set aside.
3. Mash the bananas in a separate bowl, then beat in the coconut milk, oil, honey and quinoa.
4. Fold the wet ingredients into the dry ingredients until just combined, then scrape into the tin.
5. Bake for 50 minutes or until a skewer inserted in the centre comes out clean.
6. Leave to cool on a wire rack, then slice and serve with coconut butter for spreading.

Strawberry Verrines

400 ml / 14 fl. oz / 2 cup canned coconut milk, chilled unopened

2 tbsp runny honey

1 tsp vanilla extract

250 ml / 9 fl. oz / 1 cup soya yogurt

100 g / 3 ½ oz / ¾ cup healthy granola

30 g / 1 oz / ¼ cup raw cocoa nibs

150 g / 5 oz / 1 cup strawberries, half sliced, half quartered

4 sprigs of mint

1. Open the can of coconut milk upside down and discard the thin watery layer. Scoop the thick creamy layer into a bowl and add the honey and vanilla extract.
2. Whip with an electric whisk until it reaches the consistency of whipped cream, then fold in the yogurt.
3. Divide a third of the mixture between four glasses. Mix the granola and cocoa nibs together and scatter half over the top, then arrange the sliced strawberries around the inside of the glasses.
4. Top with the rest of the coconut mixture then garnish with the rest of the granola, the quartered strawberries and mint sprigs.

MAKES: **9** | PREP TIME: **20 MINS** | COOKING TIME: **35 MINS**

Matcha Brownies

225 g / 8 oz / 1 ½ cups gluten-free plain (all-purpose) flour

½ tsp baking powder

1 ½ tbsp matcha green tea powder

1 tbsp pure cacao powder

185 g / 6 ½ oz / ¾ cup unsweetened apple puree

150 g / 5 ½ oz / ¾ cup coconut sugar

100 ml / 3 ½ fl. oz / ½ cup coconut oil, melted

75 ml / 2 ½ oz / ⅓ cup coconut milk

1 tsp vanilla extract

FOR THE ICING

100 g / 3 ½ oz / 1 cup coconut flour

1 tbsp runny honey

1. Preheat the oven to 180°C (160°C fan) / 350F / gas 4 and oil and line a 20 cm (8 in) square cake tin with greaseproof paper.

2. Mix together the flour, baking powder, matcha and cacao in a large mixing bowl and set aside.

3. Beat the rest of the ingredients together in a separate bowl then fold the wet mixture into the dry ingredients until just combined.

4. Scrape the mixture into the prepared tin and level the surface. Bake for 35 minutes or until just set in the centre. Leave to cool completely in the tin before cutting into squares.

5. Mix the coconut flour with the honey to make a thick pipeable icing, adding a few drops of water if necessary. Spoon it into a piping bag and pipe a few lines across each brownie.

SERVES: **8** | PREP TIME: **15 MINS** | COOKING TIME: **50 MINS**

Banana Bread

125 g / 4 ½ oz / 1 ¼ cups rolled porridge oats

125 g / 4 ½ oz / 1 ¼ cups ground almonds

100 g / 3 ½ oz / ½ cup coconut sugar

200 g / 7 oz / 1 ⅓ cups gluten-free plain (all-purpose) flour

3 tsp baking powder

3 very ripe bananas, mashed

1 egg, beaten

175 ml / 6 fl. oz / ⅔ cup soya milk

50 ml / 1 ¾ fl. oz / ¼ cup coconut oil, melted

sliced bananas to serve

1. Preheat the oven to 180°C (160°C fan) / 350F / gas 4 and oil and line a large loaf tin with greaseproof paper.
2. Put the oats in a food processor and blitz to a powder. Add the ground almonds, coconut sugar, flour and baking powder and blend again briefly to mix.
3. Add the bananas, egg, soya milk and coconut oil and pulse until smoothly combined, then scrape into the tin.
4. Bake for 50 minutes or until a skewer inserted in the centre comes out clean. Leave to cool completely on a wire rack before slicing and serving with sliced banana.

SERVES: **8** | PREP TIME: **30 MINS** | FREEZING TIME: **4 HOURS**

Vanilla and Blackberry Vegan Cheesecake

250 g / 9 oz / 1 ½ cups medjool dates, stoned
225 g / 8 oz / 2 ¼ cups ground almonds
450 g / 1 lb / 3 ⅓ cups raw cashew nuts, soaked overnight
800 ml / 1 pint 8 fl. oz / 4 cups canned coconut milk, (2 cans) chilled unopened
3 lemons, juiced and zest finely grated
125 ml / 4 fl. oz / ½ cup runny honey
2 tsp vanilla extract
150 g / 5 ½ oz / 1 cup blackberries

1. Soak the dates in warm water for 10 minutes, then drain and blend to a smooth paste in a food processor. Add the ground almonds and pulse until it forms a dough.
2. Line a 23 cm (9 in) round spring-form cake tin with clingfilm, then press the mixture into the base.
3. Drain the cashews and put them in the food processor. Open the cans of coconut milk upside down and discard the thin watery layer. Scoop the thick creamy layer into the food processor and add the lemon juice, zest, honey and vanilla extract.
4. Blend until very smooth, pausing to scrape down the sides occasionally.
5. Pour the cashew mixture over the base, then cover with clingfilm and freeze for at least 4 hours.
6. Remove from the freezer 20 minutes before serving. Unmould the cheesecake and top with blackberries just before serving.

SERVES: 4 | PREP TIME: 10 MINS | CHILLING TIME: 2 HOURS

Dark Chocolate Espresso Mousse

100 g / 3 ½ oz dark chocolate (100% cocoa solids)

2 ripe avocados

2 tsp good quality espresso powder

60 ml / 2 fl. oz almond milk

1 tsp vanilla extract

a pinch of salt

3 tsp date syrup

1. Break the chocolate into pieces and melt gently in a heat -proof bowl over simmering water, taking care that the water does not touch the bowl.
2. Once the chocolate has melted, place it into a blender with the remaining ingredients and blend until smooth. Add more date syrup to make it sweeter, if desired.
3. Spoon the mixture into espresso cups and refrigerate for at least 2 hours to allow the mixture to set.

SERVES: 6 | PREP TIME: 10 MINS | FREEZING TIME: 4 HOURS OR OVERNIGHT

Raspberry and Chia Lollies

225 g / 7 ½ oz / 1 ½ cups
  fresh raspberries
200 ml / 7 fl. oz / ¾ cup coconut milk
½ lemon, juiced
1 tbsp agave syrup
2 tsp chia seeds

1. Place the raspberries in a blender and blend to a puree. Pass through a sieve to remove the seeds.
2. Using a balloon whisk, beat the coconut milk for a minute or so until it is slightly thickened and well combined. Stir in the raspberry puree, syrup, lemon and chia seeds until fully mixed.
3. Pour into lolly moulds and freeze for at least 4 hours or ideally overnight, remembering to put a wooden stick in each mould.

SERVES: 12 | PREP: 30 MINS | COOK: 1 HOUR | COOL: 30 MINS | SET: 1 HOUR

Carrot Cake

200 g / 7 oz / 1 ⅓ cup self raising flour

1 tsp baking powder

1 tsp bicarbonate of soda

100 g / 3 ½ oz / 1 cup ground almonds

a pinch of salt

4 tsp mixed spice

10 g coconut oil, melted

1 large egg, beaten

2 tsp vanilla extract

150 g / 5 ¼ oz / ½ cup pure maple syrup

30 g Greek yogurt

60 ml / 2 fl. oz milk

300 g / 10 ½ oz / 2 ½ cups grated carrot

TO MAKE THE ICING

30 g Greek yogurt

250 g / 8 ¾ oz ricotta cheese

2 tsp agave syrup

1. Preheat the oven to 180°C (160°C fan) / 350F / gas 4. Grease and line a 20 cm (8 in) springform cake tin with baking paper.

2. In a large bowl combine the flour, baking powder, bicarbonate of soda, almonds, salt and mixed spice.

3. In a separate bowl, mix the oil, egg, vanilla extract, maple syrup, Greek yogurt and milk, stirring until completely smooth.

4. Make a well in the centre of the dry ingredients and gradually add the wet ingredients until combined into a thick batter, then stir in the grated carrot.

5. Pour evenly into the prepared tin and bake in the centre of the oven for 1 hour or until well risen and a skewer inserted into the centre of the cake comes out clean. Leave to cool in the tin.

6. To prepare the icing, combine the remaining ingredients in a bowl and mix until smooth. Once the cake has cooled, slice in half and add a layer of icing. Replace the top of the cake and cover with the icing.

7. Serve garnished with berries and nuts, if desired.

SERVES: 10-12 | PREP TIME: 45 MINS | COOKING TIME: 1 HOUR | CHILL: 1 HOUR

Baked Cheesecake

100 g / 3 ½ oz / ¾ cup pecans
200 g / 7 oz Medjool dates
100 g / 3 ½ oz almond butter
750 g / 1 lb 6 oz cream cheese
1 tsp vanilla extract
1 lemon, juice and zest
100 g / 3 ½ oz / ⅓ cup fruit syrup
4 eggs
2 tbsp plain flour
300 ml / 10 fl. oz / 1 ¼ cup organic soured cream

1. Preheat the oven to 160°C (140°C fan) / 325F / gas 3 and grease and line the base of a 20 cm (8 in) spring-form cake tin.
2. In a food processor, blend together the pecans, dates and almond butter until well combined. Press firmly into the base of the tin and the sides. Chill in the fridge for 30 minutes.
3. In a large bowl, gently beat together the cheese, vanilla, lemon and syrup until just combined. Add the flour and eggs, one at a time, and mix gently before folding in the soured cream.
4. Pour into the prepared base and bake in the oven for 1 hour or until set in the middle. Remove from the oven and leave to cool inside the cake tin for 2 hours before placing into the fridge for a further 4 hours or overnight.
5. To serve, carefully remove from the cake tin and place on a serving plate.
6. Top with chopped nuts, dates or seeds.

MAKES: 6 | PREP TIME: 20 MINS | COOKING TIME: 10 MINS | CHILLING: 1 HOUR

Raspberry Tartlets

100 g / 3 ½ oz / 1 cup ground almonds

1 egg, whisked

1 tbsp coconut flour

¼ tsp stevia

250 g / 8 ½ oz / 1 ⅔ cups fresh raspberries

400 ml / 13 ½ fl. oz coconut milk, refrigerated

1 tbsp fruit syrup

1 tsp vanilla extract

1 lemon, juice and zest

1. Preheat the oven to 200°C (180°C fan) / 400F / gas 6 and grease 6 tartlet cases.
2. In a large bowl, mix the ground almonds and egg and gradually add the flour, mixing until it forms a non-sticky ball of dough. Divide into 6 equal pieces and roll out to a thickness of 5 mm. Press into the cases and trim before baking for 10 minutes until crisp, then remove and leave to cool.
3. Place 200 g / 7 oz of the raspberries in a blender and blitz to a puree. Pass through a sieve to remove any seeds and set aside.
4. Carefully separate the white cream from the liquid of the coconut milk.
5. Place the cream into the bowl of a stand mixer with the syrup, vanilla and lemon. Whisk on high for 10 minutes until soft and fluffy before folding in the raspberry puree.
6. Add the whipped cream mixture to the cooled cases and top with the reserved raspberries. Chill in the fridge for at least 1 hour before serving.

MAKES: **16** | PREP TIME: **15 MINS** | COOKING TIME: **30 MINS**

Chocolate and Cranberry Brownies

50 g / 1 ½ oz dark chocolate
(100 per cent cocoa solids)
100 g / 3 ½ oz / ½ cup organic
unsalted butter
200 g / 7 oz / ⅔ cup date syrup
2 free range eggs, lightly whisked
1 tsp vanilla extract
100 g / 3 ½ oz / 1 cup ground almonds
2 tsp baking powder
pinch of salt
50 g / 1 ½ oz / ¼ cup dried cranberries

1. Preheat the oven to 180°C (160°C fan)
   / 350F / gas 4 and grease and line a
   20 cm (8 in) square tin.
2. Break the chocolate into pieces and
   melt gently with the butter in a
   heat-proof bowl over simmering
   water. Take care that the water does
   not touch the bowl.
3. Remove from the heat and allow to
   cool before beating in the date syrup,
   eggs and vanilla extract.
4. Stir in the ground almonds, baking
   powder, salt and half the cranberries.
   Mix until all the ingredients
   are combined.
5. Spread the mixture evenly in the tin
   and sprinkle over the remaining
   cranberries. Bake in the oven for
   20-25 minutes.
6. Once baked, leave to cool and cut
   into 16 even squares.

MAKES: **12** | PREP TIME: **20 MINS** | COOKING TIME: **20 MINS**

Hazelnut Cookies

100 g / 3 ½ oz / 1 cup rolled
  buckwheat flakes
150 g / 5 ½ oz / 1 cup buckwheat flour
75 g / 2 ½ oz / ⅔ cup hazelnuts, chopped
50 g / 1 ¾ oz / ½ cup desiccated coconut
100 g / 3 ½ oz / ½ cup coconut sugar
½ tsp bicarbonate of (baking) soda
125 ml / 4 ½ fl. oz / ½ cup coconut
  oil, melted

1. Preheat the oven to 180°C (160° fan) /
   350F / gas 4 and line a large baking
   tray with greaseproof paper.
2. Put all of the ingredients in a food
   processor and pulse until it forms
   a dough, adding a few tablespoons of
   water if necessary.
3. Roll the mixture into walnut-sized
   balls, then flatten them onto the
   baking tray.
4. Transfer the tray to the oven and bake
   for 20 minutes, turning round halfway
   though. Leave to cool completely on
   the tray before serving.

SERVES: **2** | PREP TIME: **1 HOUR OR OVERNIGHT**

Chia and Mango Pudding

700 ml / 24 fl. oz / 2 cups coconut milk

3 tsp coconut nectar

½ cup chia seeds

1 tsp vanilla extract

2 cardamom pods

1 medium sized mango, chopped

juice of 1 lime

1. Combine the chia seeds, coconut milk, coconut nectar, vanilla extract and cardamom pods in a bowl. Cover and refrigerate for at least an hour or overnight until the seeds have absorbed the liquid and expanded.
2. Add the lime juice to the mixture and remove the cardamom pods once ready to serve.
3. For the mango puree, set aside a small handful of the mango. Place the rest into a blender and blend until smooth. Add the small handful of chopped mango back into the puree. Sweeten with a little honey if desired.
4. To serve, pour the chia pudding into glasses and top with the mango mixture.

Snacks, Sides and Dips

SERVES: 4 | PREP TIME: 5 MINS | COOKING TIME: 30 MINS

Spiced Chickpeas

400 g / 14 oz / 2 cups canned chickpeas
1 tbsp extra virgin olive oil
½ tsp ground cumin
½ tsp ground coriander
½ tsp ground dried garlic

1. Preheat the oven to 200°C (180°C fan) / 400F / gas 6 and line a baking tray with greaseproof paper.
2. Rinse the chickpeas then drain them and dry thoroughly with kitchen paper. Toss the chickpeas with the oil, spices and a pinch of salt, then spread them out on the baking tray.
3. Roast in the oven for 35 minutes or until crisp, stirring occasionally.

SERVES: 4 | PREP TIME: 5 MINS | COOKING TIME: 15 MINS

Balsamic Baked Figs

4 fresh figs, halved
1 tbsp balsamic vinegar

1. Preheat the oven to 200°C (180°C fan) / 400F / gas 6 and line a baking tray with greaseproof paper.
2. Arrange the figs cut side up on the baking tray and drizzle with balsamic vinegar.
3. Bake the figs for 15 minutes and serve warm.

MAKES: **12** | PREP TIME: **25 MINS** | COOKING TIME: **12 MINS**

Mixed-seed Scones

150 g / 5 ½ oz / 1 cup gluten-free self-raising flour

75 g / 2 ½ oz / ½ cup buckwheat flour

1 tsp baking powder

55 g / 2 oz / ¼ cup coconut oil

75 g / 2 ½ oz / ⅓ cup mixed seeds

50 g / 1 ¾ oz / ¼ cup goji berries

2 tbsp currants

150 ml / 5 fl. oz / ⅔ cup almond milk, plus a little extra for brushing

1. Preheat the oven to 220°C (200°C fan) / 425F / gas 7 and oil a large baking sheet.
2. Sieve the flours and baking powder into a bowl and rub in the coconut oil until the mixture resembles fine breadcrumbs.
3. Mix the seeds with the goji berries and currants. Set half aside for the topping and stir the rest into the flour.
4. Stir in enough milk to bring the mixture together into a soft dough.
5. Flatten the dough with your hands on a floured work surface until 2.5 cm (1 in) thick.
6. Use a pastry cutter to cut out 12 circles and transfer them to the prepared baking sheet, then brush with almond milk and top with the rest of the seed mix.
7. Bake in the oven for 12 minutes or until golden brown and cooked through. Transfer the scones to a wire rack to cool completely.

SERVES: **4** | PREP TIME: **5 MINS**

Chilled Borscht

4 cooked beetroot, cubed

½ cucumber, peeled, seeded and cubed

600 ml / 1 pint / 2 ½ cups fresh
vegetable stock

250 ml / 9 fl. oz / 1 cup apple juice

1 tbsp cider vinegar

3 tbsp extra virgin olive oil

TO GARNISH

¼ cucumber, diced

4 radishes, diced

4 beetroot or baby chard leaves

1. Put all of the soup ingredients in
a liquidizer and blend until smooth.

2. Season to taste with salt and pepper,
then blend again.

3. Chill in the fridge until ready to
serve, then pour into glasses and
garnish with cucumber, radish and
beetroot leaves.

Kale Chips

2 tbsp extra virgin olive oil
100 g / 3 ½ oz / 3 cups kale,
  washed and dried
25 g / ¼ cup linseeds

1. Preheat the oven to 150°C (130°C fan) / 300F / gas 2.
2. Massage the oil into the kale and spread it out in a roasting tin.
3. Sprinkle with linseeds and season lightly with salt, then roast for 30 minutes,
   stirring every 10 minutes.

Date and Almond
Cacao Balls

125 g / 4 ½ oz / 1 cup blanched almonds
100 g / 3 ½ oz / 1 cup desiccated coconut
2 tbsp runny honey
75 g / 2 ½ oz / ⅓ cup almond butter
30 g / ¼ cup pure cacao powder
8 medjool dates, stoned and chopped

1. Put the almonds and coconut in a food processor and blitz until finely ground.
   Add the rest of the ingredients and pulse to form a dough.
2. Divide the dough into 12 equal pieces and roll each one into a ball.
3. Chill in the fridge for 1 hour before serving.

SERVES: 4 | **PREP TIME: 15 MINS** | **COOKING TIME: 45 MINS**

Spiced Roasted Vegetables

2 medium potatoes, halved

1 tsp cumin seeds

1 tsp coriander seeds

2 tsp thyme leaves

1 large carrot, peeled and thickly sliced

1 courgette (zucchini), halved lengthways and thickly sliced

1 small red onion, cut into wedges

1 red pepper, cut into wedges

½ small cauliflower, broken into florets

4 cloves of garlic

60 ml / 2 fl. oz / ½ cup olive oil

1. Preheat the oven to 200°C (180°C fan) / 400F / gas 6.
2. Parboil the potatoes in salted water for 8 minutes, then drain well.
3. Meanwhile, crush the cumin, coriander seeds and thyme in a pestle and mortar and stir in ½ a teaspoon of salt and a grind of black pepper.
4. Toss the vegetables with the oil in a large roasting tin and sprinkle over the spice mix.
5. Roast for 45 minutes or until tender and golden brown, stirring halfway through. Transfer the vegetables to a warm baking dish and serve immediately.

SERVES: **4** | PREP TIME: **10 MINS**

Avocado Hummus

1 small bunch flat-leaf parsley, leaves only

200 g / 7 oz / 1 cup canned chickpeas (garbanzo beans), drained

2 ripe avocados, peeled and stoned

4 tbsp extra virgin olive oil

1 tbsp tahini paste

1 lemon, juiced

1 clove of garlic, crushed

¼ tsp ground coriander

1. Reserve one parsley leaf for the garnish and put the rest in a food processor with the rest of the ingredients.
2. Blend to a smooth puree, then season to taste with salt and pepper.
3. Spoon into a bowl and garnish with the reserved parsley leaf.

SERVES: **2** | PREP TIME: **20 MINS**

Beetroot and Walnut Dip

75 g / 2 ½ oz / ½ cup walnuts, chopped
2 cooked beetroot
100 g / 3 ½ oz / ½ cup silken tofu
2 tbsp walnut oil
2 tbsp lemon juice
2 tbsp fresh dill, chopped

1. Reserve 1 tablespoon of walnuts for the garnish and soak the rest in warm water for 15 minutes.
2. Drain well, then transfer to a food processor with the beetroot, tofu, walnut oil, lemon juice and half of the dill. Blitz until very smooth, pausing to scrape down the sides occasionally.
3. Season to taste with salt and black pepper.
4. Spoon into a serving bowl and garnish with the reserved walnuts and dill.

Raw Cacao Balls

100 g / 3 ½ oz / ¾ cup hazelnuts
200 g / 7 oz / 1 ½ cups dates
2 tbsp raw cacoa, plus more for rolling
½ tsp cinnamon

1. Place the nuts in a food processor or blender and blend until they have a crumbly consistency. Add the dates, cacao and cinnamon and continue to blend until the ingredients have combined.
2. Using your hands, form the mixture into balls and roll in the additional cacao powder and place into individual cases.
3. These raw cacao balls can be stored either at room temperature or the fridge in a sealed container for up to 1 week.

SERVES: **6** | PREP TIME: **15 MINS** | COOKING TIME: **25 MINS**

Baked Parsnips with Rosemary

1 kg / 2 ½ lbs of parsnips, peeled and
   halved lengthways
1 tsp chopped fresh rosemary plus
   5 whole sprigs
3 tsp olive oil
3 whole unpeeled garlic cloves,
   lightly crushed
salt and freshly ground black pepper

1. Preheat the oven to 230°C (210°C fan) / 450F / gas 8. Mix parsnips, chopped rosemary and oil on a baking tray. Season with salt and pepper, toss to coat and spread into a single layer on baking tray.
2. Scatter the remaining rosemary sprigs and garlic cloves over the parsnips and place into the oven. Roast for 10 minutes. Turn and roast for a further 10-15 minutes until browned in places.
3. Remove from oven and discard rosemary and garlic. Season with further salt and pepper to taste and place in serving dish.
4. Garnish with fresh rosemary and serve with sour cream or Greek yogurt.

SERVES: **6** | PREP TIME: **10 MINS** | COOKING TIME: **20 MINS**

Honey Roast Carrots with Herbs

10 large carrots, sliced
2 tsp raw organic honey
1 tbsp chopped fresh rosemary
1 tbsp chopped fresh parsley
2 tbsp olive oil
salt and freshly ground black pepper

1. Heat half the oil in a large cast iron or heavy bottomed pan over a medium heat.
2. Put the remaining ingredients, except the parsley, in a bowl and toss to combine.
3. Add the carrots to the pan, allowing time to caramelize before stirring. This may have to be done in batches depending on size of the pan and will take around 20 minutes per batch.
4. Place into a serving bowl and stir through the parsley.
5. Serve immediately.

SERVES: **4** | PREP TIME: **2 HOURS 15 MINS**

Beetroot Hummus Toasts

200 g / 7 oz extra-firm tofu, in 1 piece

1 tbsp sea salt

4 tbsp extra virgin olive oil

200 g / 7 oz / 1 cup canned chickpeas (garbanzo beans), drained

2 cooked beetroot

1 tbsp tahini paste

1 lemon, juiced

1 clove of garlic, crushed

¼ tsp ground cumin

4 slices gluten-free bread, cut into triangles

2 courgettes (zucchini), sliced into ribbons with a vegetable peeler

1 small bunch flat-leaf parsley

1. Sprinkle the tofu all over with the salt, then sandwich it between two double layers of kitchen paper and weigh it down with a heavy wooden chopping board. Leave for 2 hours or preferably overnight.

2. Put half the oil in a food processor with the chickpeas, beetroot, tahini, lemon juice, garlic and cumin.

3. Blend to a smooth puree, then season to taste with salt and pepper.

4. Toast the bread and drizzle it with the rest of the oil, then top with the beetroot hummus.

5. Arrange the courgette ribbons on top, then crumble over the tofu and garnish with plenty of parsley.

SERVES: **4** | PREP TIME: **5 MINS** | COOKING TIME: **18 MINS**

Spiced Sprouts

350 g / 12 oz / 3 cups Brussels
  sprouts, trimmed

1 bay leaf

2 tbsp extra virgin olive oil

½ tsp chilli (chili) flakes

¼ tsp nutmeg, freshly grated

½ tsp mixed peppercorns,
  freshly ground

½ lemon, juiced

1. Cook the sprouts with the bay leaf in
   a large pan of salted boiling water for
   10 minutes. Drain well.

2. Heat the oil in a large sauté pan and
   add the sprouts. Cook for 5 minutes,
   turning occasionally, then sprinkle
   over the spices.

3. Sauté for 3 minutes, then drizzle with
   lemon juice and season with salt to
   taste. Serve immediately.

SERVES: **1** | PREP TIME: **10 MINS** | FREEZING TIME: **1 HOUR**

Chocolate and Banana Shake

1 ripe banana, sliced and frozen
2 tbsp raw cacoa powder
1 tbsp organic almond butter
100 ml / 3 ½ fl. oz / ½ cup almond milk
1 tsp chia seeds
1 tsp raw cacao nibs

1. Place the banana, raw cacao powder, almond butter and almond milk into a blender or food processor and blend until smooth. If too thick, add more milk until desired consistency achieved.
2. Top with the chia seeds, cacao nibs and slices of fresh banana and serve.

Raw Rainbow Salad

50 g / 1 ¾ oz / ¼ cup quinoa, cooked and drained

1 tsp chia seeds

½ lemon, juiced

¼ small red cabbage, shredded

50 g / 1 ½ oz baby spinach

100 g / 3 ½ oz / ½ cup sweetcorn

1 carrot, cut into small batons

1 red pepper, diced

50 g / 1 ¾ oz cherry tomatoes, halved

1 fresh basil leaf

1. Combine the quinoa with the chia seeds and lemon juice, place into the bottom of a mason jar or tall glass.
2. Gradually top with each of the other ingredients in order to create an attractive rainbow effect.
3. Top with the basil leaf.

Roasted Pepper and Caperberry Crostini

3 red peppers

2 tbsp extra virgin olive oil

2 tbsp flat-leaf parsley, chopped

75 g / 2 ½ oz / ½ cup pickled caperberries

1 seeded wholegrain baguette, sliced on the diagonal

1 clove of garlic, halved

1. Preheat the grill to its highest setting. Grill the peppers for
2. 20 minutes, turning occasionally, until blacked and blistered all over. Transfer the peppers to a mixing bowl and cover tightly with cling film. Leave to steam for 20 minutes.
3. When the peppers are cool enough to handle, peel off the skins and tear them into strips. Dress the peppers with the oil and a pinch of salt and pepper, then toss them with the parsley and caperberries.
4. Grill the baguette slices until lightly toasted, then rub the cut surfaces with the garlic clove.
5. Pile the peppers and caperberries on top and serve immediately.

Camembert Bites

4 slices wholemeal bread, crust removed
100 g / 3 ½ oz Camembert, sliced
4 tsp cranberry sauce
1 handful of chopped nuts

1. Place the bread on plates and top with the sliced cheese and a spoonful of cranberry sauce.
2. Sprinkle over the chopped nuts and serve immediately.
3. Great as a quick snack.

Courgette and Carrot Fritters

500 g / 1 lb 2 oz courgettes (zucchini)
200 g / 7 oz carrots
1 tbsp plain flour
2 eggs lightly beaten
30 g / ¼ cup oatmeal
4 spring onions (scallions), finely chopped
1 tsp chia seeds
1 tsp flax seeds
sea salt and ground black pepper
rapeseed oil to cook

1. Grate the courgettes and carrots and place in a colander over the sink with a pinch of salt and leave to drain for 30 minutes. Place into a tea towel and squeeze out any remaining liquid and place into a bowl.
2. Add the remaining ingredients to the bowl and combine well adding a little more seasoning.
3. In a non-stick frying pan, heat enough oil to lightly coat the base of the pan on a medium-high heat. When hot, add spoonfuls of the mixture to the pan and flatten with a spatula. Cook for a couple of minutes on each side until golden brown. Keep some warm in the oven whilst you cook the rest of the batches.
4. Place onto kitchen roll to collect any remaining oil and serve hot with a dip of your choice.

Rye Toast with Avocado

2 slices of rye bread
½ avocado, sliced
1 tsp sesame oil
1 tsp sesame seeds
½ lemon, juice only
black pepper

1. Lightly toast the rye bread and drizzle with oil before topping with the sliced avocado.
2. Squeeze over the lemon juice and top with the sesame seeds and a pinch of pepper.
3. Serve immediately.

Pear and Honey Bruschetta

2 slices multi-grain bread
150 g / 5 ¼ oz cottage cheese
½ conference pear, ripe and sliced
30 g walnut halves
30 g raw honey

1. Heat a griddle pan until smoking and toast the bread on each side.
2. Place the toasted bread on serving plate and top with the cottage cheese, pear slices and walnuts.
3. Drizzle over the raw honey and serve.

SERVES: 4 | PREP TIME: 10 MINS | COOKING TIME: 20 MINS

Spiced Roast Cauliflower

1 large cauliflower, chopped into even bite-sized pieces

4 garlic cloves, unpeeled slightly crushed

1 tsp cumin seeds, lightly crushed

1 tsp turmeric

2 tbsp olive oil

1 lemon, juice and zest

1. Preheat the oven to 200°C (180°C fan) / 400F / gas 6.
2. Combine the ingredients in a large bowl and toss to coat the cauliflower. Spread evenly on a baking tray and place in the oven for 20 minutes, turning after 10 minutes.
3. Remove when evenly browned and slightly al dente.
4. Serve with a fragrant green salad or lamb.

Index